From A to Zamboni

The Alphabet, Blackhawks® Style!

Written by
Jennifer Grocki

Illustrated by
Andy Lendway

From A to Zamboni®
The Alphabet, Blackhawks Style!

Copyright © 2014 by Jennifer Grocki

Illustrations Copyright © 2014 by Andy Landway

All Rights Reserved

Team Kidz Inc.

P.O. Box 2111

Voorhees, NJ 08043

ISBN 10: 0-9793833-6-6

ISBN 13: 978-0-9793833-6-6

Dedication

In loving memory of my mother Judy, who had a passion for life,
literature, and hockey, and to my niece Lilly and nephew Jack

in hopes that they follow in her footsteps.

- JG

For Steve, Chris and Tony! Also for Sam and Kim, new Hawks fans.

Love you all!

- AL

A is for Anthem, we sing with great pride,

B is for Bench, where we sit side by side.

C is for Coach, who stands tall and proud,

D is for Defense, through which no goal's allowed.

E is for Elbows, that can't get too high,

F is for Fans, who watch us fly by.

G is for Goalie, who guards our team's net,

H is for Hat Trick, we'll never forget!

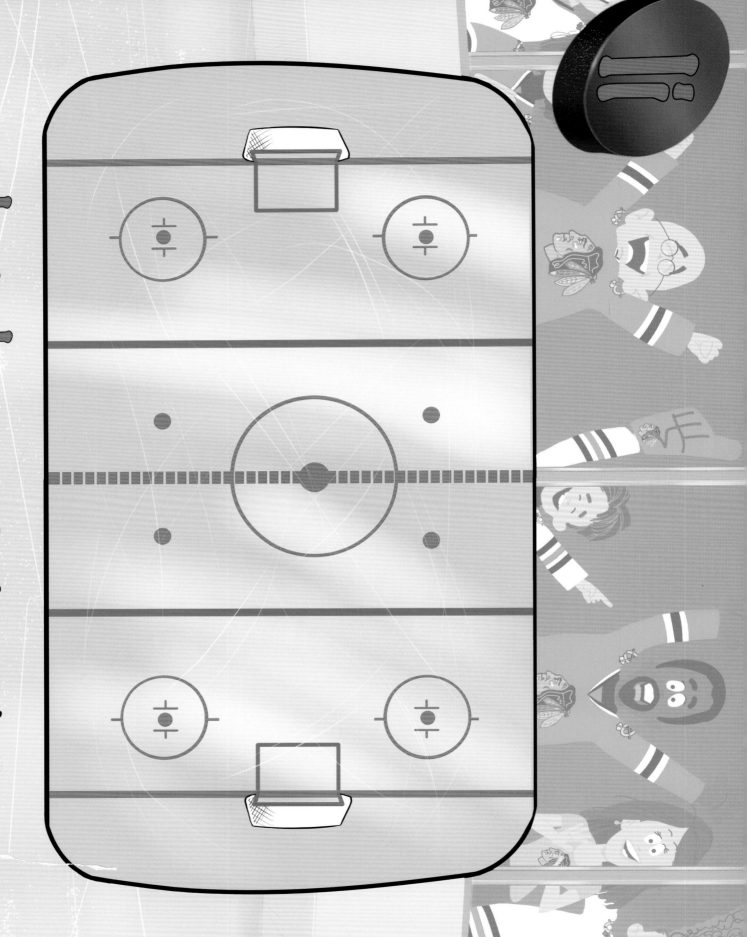

I is for Ice, we can't play without,

J is for Jersey, worn with honor, no doubt.

K is for Kicking, we know we can't do.

L is for Linesman, whose eyes are on you.

M is for Mask, which we wear on our face,

N is for Net, where the puck finds its place.

O is for Obstruction, which gets you the door,

P is for Puck, we pass, shoot, and we score!

Q is for Quiet, when we don't have the lead,

R is for Red Line, we cross with great speed.

S is for Stick, we handle with care,

T is for Team, who will always be there.

U is for Underdog, which we've all been before,

V is for Victory, the moment we score!

W is for Winger, who passes just right,

X is for Xs, used to plan for game night.

Y is for Yippee, you yell with a friend,

Z is for Zamboni machine, making ice at The End!

THE END

Autographs

Autographs